I Y'AMZ

WHAT I AM

GOD, POPEYE & ME

SHAWN D. RUSSELL

YBD Your Best Dash®
PUBLISHING

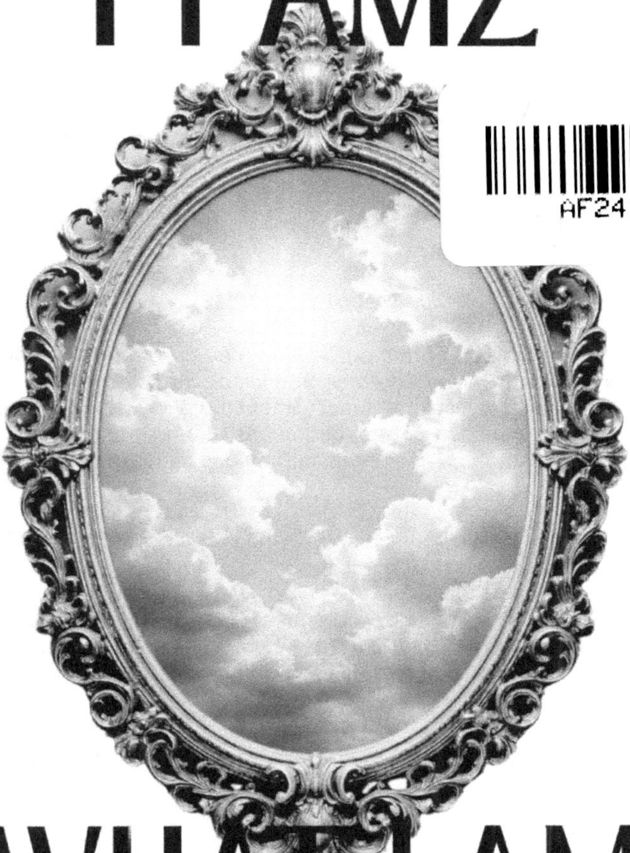

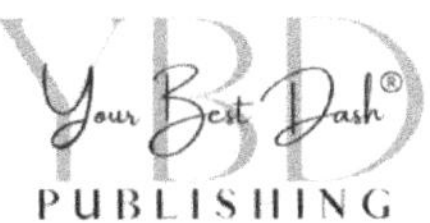

All emphasis in Scripture quotations (italics or boldface) has been added by the author.

ISBN 978-1-966229-06-3 (paperback)

Cover design by Your Best Dash®

Published by Your Best Dash®
www.yourbestdash.com

Printed in the United States

This book is dedicated to all those who are searching for their identity and their place in the Kingdom of God.

To those who struggle with who they are. To those who carry their father's name and are still unsure of what that means.

This book is also dedicated to the memory of my late father, Alonzo O. Russell, whom I miss dearly. Dad, I did it!

TABLE OF CONTENTS

INTRODUCTION

Go therefore and make disciples of all the nations, baptizing them in the name of the Father and of the Son and of the Holy Spirit. (Matthew 28:19 NKJV)

GOD. POPEYE. AND ME? Yes, you read it correctly. There are no typos or misprints here. The title is correct. God is the all-powerful, all-knowing, omnipresent Creator of the universe. He is the maker of heaven and earth and all things in between. Popeye is the larger-than-life, spinach-eating, tattoo-wearing comic character. Then, there is me, perhaps more accurately, the total me, comprised of every decision and experience: the good, bad, and indifferent.

All three: God, Popeye, and I, are connected by a series of comparisons and truths. The Holy Bible and my imagination serve as the glue for this rather unique adventure. Oh, please do not underestimate the power of the connections here. The power surging through this connectivity may surprise you and even overload your circuits. Prayerfully and with all due diligence, you will not only see the connections but also experience them as I did when I first received this download.

If you're like most people, you've probably spent plenty of time wondering how others see you. Lord knows I've done that, too. But have you ever stopped to think about how God sees you? I've wondered about that as well. I'm guilty as charged. If you're a follower of Christ, that means you're part of the Church. So, here's another question: how does God see the Church? One more question: how do people view "the Church"? I'm not talking about the building where we gather to worship, but the body of believers itself. How does God view His very own people?

Yeah, yeah, yeah. You're probably already asking the question: what does this have to do with God, Popeye, and me? Patience, I'm getting there. Before we cast off on that venture, please allow me to set some groundwork for the journey.

This book is the result of God using my imagination to convey some rather interesting truths. Popeye and his crew of misfits make a great comparison to the body of Christ. It's truly something to behold. If I've done my job well, you'll finish this book with a lighthearted and enlightened I Y'amz What I Am—a play on one of Popeye's famous statements: "I yams what I yams!"

I know some will say it's wrong to compare the Church to a cartoon character. I mean, we're not talking about Superman or Captain America; we're talking about Popeye. Some may even say it's blasphemous, but rest assured, the Church has more in common with the runt Popeye than with any of those other heroes. Perhaps you'll see it the way God showed it to me. Then, it might change your perspective and maybe even your life.

Way back in May of 2005, God gave me what I call a "revelatory download." I was amazed then, and even more so now, by how the information was deposited. I was traveling and talking with my best friend about our identity in Christ when it happened! The download transpired, and I knew I was on to something. Just as Jesus taught in parables during His earthly mission, I understood that He was using a similar approach with me.

My prayer and goal are simple: to impart that same understanding to you. We must not only understand but also act. The world stands at a crossroads, and the Church must become what God intended all along.

Even if only one person receives this revelation, though I believe more will, then I've done my job well. To be effective in shaping the world, the Church must rise from mediocrity and compromise to become a kingdom organism of substantial force and value.

Chapter 1

POPEYE

POPEYE MAY BE ONE of the most recognizable cartoon characters in the world. He's universal. No matter what continent you visit, his impact has been felt in some way.

Have you ever stopped to think about the connection between Popeye the Sailor Man and the Church of the living God? Probably not, but there is one. As I mentioned earlier, I was on a trip when God gave me this revelation. He allowed me to replay scenes from the cartoon in my mind. I watched as Popeye was beaten to a pulp by Bluto, while the voice of his love interest, Olive Oyl, cried out, "Oh, Popeye! Help, Popeye! Help!" As I watched the cartoon parade in my mind, the Holy Spirit enlightened me how this would play out. Each character from the Popeye cartoon carries its own symbolism pertaining to the Christian walk. Popeye himself is symbolic of the Church. However, he does not represent the idealistic church, but rather the real church of our current time. We will start here.

Popeye is a sailor of small build who is more recognized for his characteristics than his character. A physical description of Popeye is as follows: he is a short man with a blind eye, overdeveloped forearms, and a bug-like, gravelly voice. He gets into trouble and eats spinach to gain the strength needed to fight his enemies, an underdog of sorts. But have we simply overlooked the obvious? Popeye's differences are the source of his strengths.

It is often assumed that people of short stature are inferior. However, we cannot base our understanding of this character on mere physical appearance, especially as it relates to the Church. According to sources, Popeye was 34 years old when he was first introduced. He stood 5 feet 6 inches tall and weighed a whopping 158 pounds. In relation to the Church, Popeye's height symbolizes the "underdog" capacity in which the world views the Church. But the Church of Jesus Christ as an underdog is not what the Lord had in mind.

Everything in the world seems to be going crazy and it feels as if we are going to hell in a handbasket, but where is the Church? Select leaders are trying to get the Church to take an effective position in our society. However, just like Popeye, this has come up against much opposition.

Surprisingly, it appears that most it is from within the Church itself. How is it that the chosen bride of Christ is considered ineffective and weak in a time when God is pouring out His Spirit upon all flesh? Torn by scandal and internal conflicts, the Church, as the world sees it, has too many problems of its own to serve as a balm for society. There is a healing balm for the world, but why does it remain hidden? A light that is hidden cannot reach those who need it most. The Church is the answer.

David and Popeye have something in common. David was once King of Israel—a man with flaws, but after God's own heart. As a child, he was considered the runt of the family. He was so disregarded by his family that he was not even included in the gathering of sons by his father, Jesse, at the request of Samuel the Prophet. Most are familiar with the story found in 1 Samuel 16.

David's story continues to gain traction in 1 Samuel 17, when the infamous confrontation of David and Goliath comes to a head. Though he was the least likely, David knew that there was a giant that had to be dealt with. He allowed God to develop and cultivate the giant within him to do the work that no one else was willing to do. Before his encounter with Goliath, David had honed his skills by fighting lions and bears while tending to his father's sheep. He would eventually go to battle against Goliath with the same tools he used daily. Like David, will the Church allow God to cultivate the warrior within that is needed to slay the giants in the earth today? Will the real Church arise and stand head and shoulders above the opposition? Will it be the city that sits on a hill, refusing to be hidden?

Let's not get it twisted. For years, the Church has been guilty of portraying David as the underdog in this story, but nothing could be further from the truth. David was no underdog. The Bible makes it clear that he was highly skilled with his weapons.

Saul answered David, "You can't go and fight this Philistine. You're too young and inexperienced – and he's been at this fighting business since before you were born." David said, "I've been a shepherd, tending sheep for my father. Whenever a lion or a bear came and took a lamb from the flock, I'd go after it, knock it down and rescue the lamb. If it turned on me, I'd grab it by the throat, wring its neck, and kill it. Lion or bear, it made no difference – I killed it. (1 Samuel 17:33-35 MSG)

David knew how to handle both his staff and his slingshot. He was deadly with what he had perfected in practice. He killed both lions and bears— "oh my." The slingshot was not a little kid's toy; it was a weapon—deadly and accurate in the hands of a skilled slinger. The stones were not the size of pebbles; rather, they averaged the size of a fist, which also explains why he only picked up five. Any more than that, and they would have interfered with his momentum. Look at his words in the above Scripture. He knew what he could do, but he had to spend time convincing King Saul and his own brothers that he was up to the task at hand.

So, here we are comparing the Church to Popeye and Popeye to David, but why are we comparing them? How does it all fit together? Isn't it obvious? David was tending to his father's sheep before he was anointed king. Afterward, he went back to tending his father's sheep. He was putting in the work. He was perfecting his gifts. He was building his confidence as he performed his due diligence. He was taking care of the sheep while, at the same time, still being denied and ignored.

Now the Spirit of the LORD had left Saul, and
the LORD sent a tormenting
that filled him with depression and fear.
(1 Samuel 16:14 NLT)

David also spent time serving. While King Saul was being tormented with depression and fear that the LORD allowed, David, who had been anointed to be king, was also anointed to play the harp to soothe the savage beast within the king. The point that I want us to see here is that David put in the work and allowed God to take him through situation after situation. He did this to build the warrior within him, so that one day, he could deal with the warrior that would come against him.

The Church must be willing to do the work required to handle the enemies that have and will come up against it. However, our track record in this particular area is not a good one. We are losing ground to an enemy that does not have an advantage. David and Goliath both stood on the middle ground in the Valley of Elah. David had the upper hand, which is why he won.

The Church must stop approaching situations without wisdom like Popeye does. Instead, we must be more like David and face them as warriors. When we act like Popeye, we are caught off guard and respond like the underdog. However, if we are like David, we can confront every giant knowing that we have the upper hand.

STANDING TALL

Standing at only 5 feet 6 inches tall, Popeye reminds me of a biblical character named Zacchaeus when it comes to height. I cannot help but compare the two. Zacchaeus was a wealthy Jewish tax collector in the time of Jesus. He, too, was short in stature—so short, in fact, that the Bible says when Jesus was visiting Jericho, Zacchaeus could not see Him over the crowds. So, Zacchaeus chose to run ahead and climb a tree to get a good look at Jesus as he passed by.

Jesus entered Jericho and was passing through. A man was there by the name of Zacchaeus; he was a chief tax collector and was wealthy. He wanted to see who Jesus was, but because he was short, he could not see over the crowd. So he ran ahead and climbed a sycamore-fig tree to see him, since Jesus was coming that way. When Jesus reached the spot, he looked up and said to him, "Zacchaeus, come down immediately. I must stay at your house today.

(Luke 19:1-5 NKJV)

I wonder if, like Zaccheus in the tree, the Church has elevated itself to a position that makes room for it to look down on Christ, all the while observing what is going on around Him—to see much but do little. If you've noticed, many churches today have moved away from Christ's teachings in favor of a more relaxed, all-inclusive approach. In an effort not to alienate anyone, some have even embraced an antichrist spirit.

Notice that when Jesus arrived on the scene, He told Zacchaeus to come down immediately because He wanted to spend time with him. Perhaps God is saying the same thing to the Church through this book: "Come down from the place where you have lifted yourself above others—maybe higher than you ought to be.

Humble yourselves before the Lord, and he will lift you up in honor.

(James 4:10 NLT)

Many believers have elevated themselves to high and lofty positions, looking down on the Word of God, looking down on Jesus, and all that is holy. Jesus is warning the Church: "Hurry up and come down."

At this very moment, the Church appears to many to be both overrated and undervalued at the same time. The world is in crisis mode, with new sicknesses and diseases spreading. Now more than ever, the Church must arise and be a source of hope for a world that is desperately searching for it.

Throughout the storyline, Popeye's enemies would often look at his small stature as permission to attack him. They believed they could easily defeat him because they failed to take his true abilities into consideration. Has the Church allowed itself to be presented in the same way? Is the Church overlooking a world in crisis?

There is no doubt that God never intended for the Church to be an underdog of any sort. We have the authority given to us through Christ to be effective and to be the change needed in the world. We must walk in that authority, showing God's perfect love to those who need it most. If the Church is not willing to walk in its identity and authority, many people will suffer and never know the saving power of Jesus.

We, the Church, cannot afford to be idle during this time when God is allowing us the opportunity to reach the masses. Are we adapting to the mindset of the ten of the twelve spies sent into Canaan? They saw themselves as inferior to the inhabitants of the land. Does the Church see itself in the same way?

> *There we saw the giants (the descendants of Anak came from the giants); and we were like grasshoppers in our own sight, and so we were in their sight.* (Numbers 13:33 NKJV).

LET'S GET PHYSICAL

Though Popeye is shorter than the average person, he can summon great strength in times of need. Popeye is not often seen working out, but the evidence suggests that he has. One of the most notable features of Popeye's physical appearance is his massively overdeveloped forearms. They seem symbolic of being overworked in some areas while neglected in others. I found this particularly interesting when the LORD reminded me of the anchor tattoos on both of Popeye's forearms.

Anchors aweigh! An anchor is a heavy object designed to secure a vessel to the bottom of the sea. It is also one of the many symbols associated with Christ. It is possible that Popeye's anchor tattoos could represent the Church being anchored in works rather than in the Word of God.

For by grace you have been saved through
faith, and not of yourselves. It is the gift of
GOD, not of works, lest anyone should boast.
(Ephesians 2:8-9 NLT)

Our salvation is not based upon our works but simply upon the work that Christ did on the cross. Granted, we do have to perform certain works for the gospel of Christ to be spread throughout the earth. The Church has all kinds of programs to reach those who need to hear the gospel. However, our salvation is not based upon those works. We should not find our security in our works, but rather in our hope.

This hope we have as an anchor of the soul,

both sure and steadfast, and

which enters the Presence behind the veil.

(Hebrews 6:19 NLT)

Let us be reminded that the anchor tattoos on Popeye's arms should reflect the surety of our hope, not the work that we do. No matter what, our hope must be in the very presence of God. An anchor is used to keep a ship from drifting in deep waters. You don't see ships using anchors in shallow water. We must be anchored in the deep things of

God. We cannot spend too much time focusing on minor issues within the Church; we must be willing to launch into the deep.

If you are familiar with the cartoon, you know that whenever Popeye eats spinach, he flexes his arms and legs, stretching those anchors. In the same way, we must stretch our hope and faith in the process.

SEEING EYE TO EYE

Another aspect of Popeye's appearance that I would like to focus on is his eyes—or should I say his eye? It is unclear whether he is completely blind in one eye or simply squinting. I have seen cartoons depicting both. Nonetheless, Popeye essentially operates with limited vision. Let us try this experiment: close one eye and look around. What do you see? Not nearly as much as when using both eyes. Like Popeye, the Church is operating with a limited view of things. The entire view is distorted. You may be able to see what is directly in front of you but not able to see the entire picture.

And if your eye causes you to sin, gouge it out. It's better to enter the Kingdom of God with only one eye than to have two eyes and be thrown into hell. (Mark 9:47 NLT)

This Scripture reference addresses willful sin. It should also apply to willfully ignoring the Scriptures. The problem here is that the Church cannot seem to take on the issues it faces. We are so busy gouging out each other's eyes instead of covering one another to ensure healing. Have you ever had your eyes dilated? I have. It was horrible. I could not see anything clearly. I must have looked like Popeye as I squinted in vain. I had to wait before driving because everything was distorted. Had I driven right away, I would have been a danger to everyone around me.

If the Church would truly open its eyes to the world around us, we would see how desperately people need our Savior. We can no longer perceive the world as "us versus them." Now is the time to see it for what it is—a world full of sick people who are tired of being sick and tired. They are people in need of a hospital. The Scriptures must guide everything we do, setting the boundaries within which we operate. Too many people are turning to every other option because we have not presented the gospel of Christ in a way that speaks to their hearts.

According to Google, there are more than 200 distinct Christian bodies in the United States alone. That's more than 200 different interpretations and views on how to apply Scripture. How did we get to the place where there are over 200 denominations in the U.S.? It must be because people want to "see" the Word of God in their own way. Each denomination is made up of people with differing thoughts, ideas, talents, skills, and varying degrees of faith. That's more than 200 ways of getting things right—or wrong—more than 200 ways of walking different paths into different "truths."

If only the Church would simply declare the Word of Christ and operate in love and unity. It's no wonder that unbelievers have such a difficult time believing in the Bible when the Church itself struggles to declare the truth of God's Word.

There is a quote by Lee Atwater that says, “Perception is reality.” My personal quote is, “Perception is reception!” Essentially, both statements express the same idea—that how a person perceives something is how they will receive it. As the saying goes, “It’s their truth.”

Popeye’s limited vision leaves him susceptible to making poor judgment calls. It would be great if Jesus could put some mud on Popeye’s eyes to correct his vision. However, Popeye is not real, but the Church is. I pray that we would begin to see the world with the same view that God does.

He said to his disciples, “The harvest is great, but the workers are few.” (Matthew 9:37 NLT)

Popeye’s focus is usually on saving his beloved Olive Oyl whenever she gets into trouble. Though he may be trapped by any of his enemy’s schemes, he always finds a way to rescue her. In the same way, the harvest represents the field of unclaimed souls. The Church must have a heart to go to the nations and proclaim the gospel of Jesus Christ in love. Just as Popeye goes to great lengths to save Olive Oyl from the enemy, the Church must be willing to go above and beyond to reach the lost, to proclaim the gospel to those in need of the Savior.

Now as they went out of Jericho, a great multitude followed Him. And behold, two blind men sitting by the road, when they heard that Jesus was passing by, cried out, saying, "Have mercy on us, O Lord, Son of David! Then the multitude warned them that they should be quiet; but they cried out all the more, saying, "Have mercy on us, O Lord, Son of David!" So Jesus stood still and called them, and said, "What do you want Me to do for you?" They said to Him, "Lord, that our eyes may be opened." So Jesus had compassion and touched their eyes. And immediately their eyes received sight, and they followed Him."

(Matthew 20:29-34 NKJV)

There were two blind men sitting on the side of the road as Jesus was leaving Jericho. This was a common place for the blind and crippled to gather, begging alms from those who passed by. Though they could not see, they could hear that Jesus was passing their way. They knew who He was, and it was probably their one and only chance to be healed. The Bible says they said, “Have mercy on us, O Lord, Son of David!” (Matthew 20:30, NKJV)

They could probably hear better than those with sight. Something remarkable happens in the human body when it is denied one of its natural senses: the other senses compensate for what is missing. They could hear Him coming and the voices of the people calling out to Jesus. They knew they had to make their prayer heard. The Bible says that they “CRIED OUT!”

The phrase “cry out” means “to make a loud inarticulate sound expressing fear, pain, or grief” or “to say something loudly in an excited or anguished tone of voice” (Oxford Languages, Google Dictionary).

This was no ordinary outcry. It was a prayer, an extremely specific prayer at that. In Matthew 20:30, "O" was the word used in place of "Dear" when formally addressing someone. The word "Lord" refers to someone having power, authority, or influence, a master or ruler. "Son of David" refers to Christ being the total fulfillment of the prophecy of the seed of David. Primarily, the term "Son of David" is more than just a title; it is a statement of genealogy that physically flows through forty-two generations. It is the title of the Messiah. When people referred to Jesus as the Son of David, they were, in fact, declaring that He was the long-awaited promised Deliverer of the Jewish nation, the fulfillment of Old Testament prophecies.

The fact that they did not call Him Jesus lets us know that their prayer "O" was not about Jesus the man. It was, instead, an acknowledgment of His holy power, authority, and influence. They were declaring His position as Master of the universe. As Lord, they knew that He had the power and authority to speak to their situation. He had authority to speak into the spirit realm—to position angels for victory and cast out demons. If He was indeed the Deliverer as they believed Him to be, He had the authority to set them free. It was a legal appeal to His royal position as King, knowing that whenever a king makes a declaration, it cannot be undone. They were on to something!

There was a huge crowd following Jesus and the disciples as they were leaving Jericho. They were the ones who told the blind men to be quiet. That was then; this is now and not much has changed. People following Jesus are still telling others in need of a breakthrough to be quiet. But it did not stop the blind men. The Bible says that they cried out, "Have mercy on us, O Lord, Son of David!"

The Church is much like those blind men, sitting on the side of the road, begging alms from people but needing to cry out, "Have mercy on us, O Lord, Son of David!" The Church has been overlooking the harvest because we have been blind. We have limited vision and must have our sight restored in order to focus on those who have been invisible for far too long. There must be a shift in the vision of today's church.

Otherwise, we will continue to concentrate on those already saved while ignoring the lost.

NOTES

CHAPTER 2

WORD OF MOUTH

POPEYE HAD A long list of catchphrases that I would like to touch on. I will not go through the complete list, but I will highlight some of the ones that caught my ear and eye.

For by your words you will be justified, and by your words you will be condemned.
(Matthew 12:37 NKJV)

Death and life are in the power of the tongue, and those who love it will eat its fruit.
(Proverbs 18:21 NKJV)

Not only is Popeye remembered for his physical appearance, but also for the words that come from his mouth. Before diving into the meat of this chapter, I would like to define a few words so that we can better understand what is taking place before us.

According to Oxford Languages, "profession" is defined as "an act of declaring that one has a particular feeling or quality, especially when this is not the case." Likewise, confession is defined as "a formal statement admitting that one is guilty of a crime" or "a statement setting out essential religious doctrine."

I have known several sailors in my lifetime. Many of my relatives were in the U.S. Navy. With Popeye being a sailor, it's only fitting that we address his use of certain words and phrases. He was truly befitting of the saying "cuss like a sailor," and his choice of words may have contributed to many of the predicaments he found himself in.

Part of a sailor's environment is not only the boat itself but also where that boat spends most of its time when not in use—the dock. The docks during the time of Popeye's release were made from wooden timbers. These timbers were similar to the wooden telephone poles we use today and were submerged in water. The timber formed the main foundation of the pier system. The dock was supported by the timbers that lay beneath the vision of the everyday person.

According to Oxford Languages, "shiver" is defined as "(of a person or animal) shake slightly and uncontrollably as a result of being cold, frightened or excited," and "timber" is defined as "wood suitable for building or for carpentry."

Popeye made famous the quote: "Shiver me timbers!" If "shiver" means to shake slightly or uncontrollably because of fear, and timber was the wood used for building the foundation from which he would stand, then Popeye was literally saying that his foundation was being shaken. Am I reading too much into this? I do not think so. Neither should you. I will show you why.

Popeye often made this confession whenever he was in a crisis. Whether he was under attack by Bluto, Brutus, or some other adversary, he would mutter these convicting words as if there was nothing else that he could say or do. As believers, if we're not anchored in the Word of God, we, too, can find our foundations shaken in crises, challenges, or distress.

Paul emphasized the importance of having a stable foundation.

According to the grace of God which was given to me, as a wise master builder I have laid the foundation, and another builds on it. But let each one take heed how he builds on it. For no other foundation can anyone lay than that which is laid, which is Jesus Christ.

(1 Corinthians 3:10-11 NKJV)

If our foundation is shaken, then we have no stability or balance in our lives. Balance is of the utmost importance. When our foundation is unstable and we are off balance, everything around us is at risk of falling from its place of importance. Should that happen, our entire world and the value of everything in it would change.

Without our skeletal system, we would simply be blobs with no shape or basis for support. Our ribs not only provide structure, but they are also a vital part of our survival. They exist for protection. Without our ribs, our entire respiratory system would fall into chaos. Our hearts and lungs would move around freely, leading to suffocation and heart failure.

The function of the ribs goes far beyond protection; they are essential for life.

The Bible says that the Church is the bride of Christ, and it reminds us that Jesus is not returning for a blemished bride.

> *Husbands, love your wives, just as Christ also loved the church and gave Himself for her, that He might sanctify and cleanse her with the washing of water by the word, that He might present her to Himself a glorious church, not having spot or wrinkle or any such thing, but that she should be holy and without blemish.* (Ephesians 5:25-27 NKJV)

I know that the above Scripture usually serves as a reference for how husbands should love their wives, but it also provides clear insight into the well-being and presentation of the bride. Shaken brides do not make it to the altar. They abandon the groom, breaking the promises of anticipated vows and leaving behind an unfulfilled union.

The Church, like our sailor Popeye, must be incredibly careful about the words we use and the way in which we use them. Popeye often operated with negative confessions, and the results were usually a hindrance to his mission. If he declared that his foundation was shaken, then he would soon find himself dealing with that very scenario. Why do we speak death into a situation and then act surprised when it dies?

The same principle applies regardless of who is speaking. There are laws at work in our universe that apply to everyone. Individual belief does not exempt anyone from them. Millions of non-Christians live by godly principles yet leave God out of the equation.

Popeye's second catchphrase is remarkably similar to the first in that it also projects negativity. Our hero would cry out the troubling statement, "Blow me down." This is certainly another invitation for disaster. Once again, the structure of his security is being challenged. These negative words frame the world in which he lives.

"That's all I can stand, 'cause I can't stands no more," is a third catchphrase filled with words of defeat and negativity. Let us not forget that even though Popeye is a cartoon character, he still serves here as a point of comparison with the Church.

Let us think about it for a moment. We are all here for a purpose. There is no mistake about that. God knows what He is doing. The challenge lies in our willingness to align ourselves with His Word and become His promise to the earth and the people in it.

Much like Popeye, when challenged to fulfill our purpose, we often assume that the pressure is coming from Satan rather than from God. So, in futility, we attempt to bind Satan when it is God pushing us toward our destiny. We must pay close attention to the words we speak, understanding the power they carry. Our tongues are directly connected to our central nervous system. Whenever we speak, whether words of affirmation or negativity—our bodies respond, putting those words into action.

It is the Spirit who gives life; the flesh profits nothing. The words that I speak to you are spirit, and they are life.

(John 6:63 NKJV)

Therefore, keep watch over your mouth and the words that you use. Negative confession will always lead to condemnation, while profession of the Word of God will always promote and propel you toward your destiny.

According to Britannica.com, life is living matter and has certain attributes, including responsiveness, growth, metabolism, energy transformation, and reproduction. While it is defined as a noun, like other entities, it may be more accurate to think of it as a verb, reflecting its essential status as a process.

Words are spirit. They are life. They have the power to transform anything. In fact, they are so powerful that the universe is still expanding based on one word spoken by God thousands of years ago. This same power applies to our lives today. So, no matter how tired you may be or how bad your situation is, remember God's Word still works. It always has and it always will.

The words of a man's mouth are deep waters;
The wellspring of wisdom is a flowing brook.
(Proverbs 18:4 NKJV)

Brood of vipers! How can you, being evil, speak good things? For out of the abundance of the heart the mouth speaks.
(Matthew 12:34 NKJV)

For by your words you will be justified, and by your words you will be condemned.
(Matthew 12:37 NKJV)

Let no corrupt word proceed out of your mouth, but what is good for necessary edification, that it may impart grace to the hearers.
(Ephesians 4:29 NKJV)

We can go on for pages about the undeniable power of words. However, when it comes down to it, the Church must adjust what we are saying to align more closely with the Holy Bible. We must not only change what we are saying but to whom we are saying it. Mixed messages are certainly being sent forth during a time when we must be specific and intentional about what we are saying.

Remember when I made mention of the more than 200 different denominations in the US? Each one is saying something the other is not. This must change for there to be a unified body of believers. Otherwise, the church will not resemble the beautiful bride described in Ephesians 5. Instead, it will more likely resemble the bride of Frankenstein.

NOTES

CHAPTER 3

BLUTO THE TERRIBLE

A ROGUES GALLERY is a compilation of descriptions, methods of operation (modi operandi), hiding places, and names of criminals and their known associates. Every hero has one. Not only does each hero have a Rogues Gallery, but they also have at least one enemy who stands out as their most prominent and worst foe—their arch-nemesis. There are no exceptions to this rule. Batman has the Joker, and Spiderman has the Green Goblin. For Jesus, it was sin. And for our hero in question, Popeye, it's Bluto. If you're familiar with the cartoon, you may be saying, "What about Brutus?" Rest assured, Brutus has his place as well.

First introduced to the Thimble Theatre comic strip in 1932 as a one-time character, "Bluto the Terrible" would later become the main enemy of Popeye. Later, the character was renamed Brutus because of a technicality, and there was more than just a name change. Though Bluto and Brutus look almost identical, they are distinct characters. That subtle difference can make or break you in a time of war.

Your enemies may have different appearances but still fall under the same category. If your struggle is with sweets, you'll note that cake, ice cream, pie, and doughnuts are four distinctly different items; yet they all fall under the same category of sweets. The king snake and coral snake both share the same color scheme of red, black, and yellow. However, one is non-venomous, and the other is deadly. A poem I heard on a TV show once said it like this: "Red on black, venom lack. Red on yellow, kill a fellow." While the poem is intended to help people tell the difference, for some, the only good snake is a dead snake. Bluto and Brutus are both enemies of Popeye. Following the pattern of this book, let us break each down and identify its corresponding place in our comparison with the Church.

The name Bluto suggests the very thing most people deal with daily. It is believed to have originated from the word "bloat." Bloat is defined in Dictionary.com as both a noun and a verb, bloat refers to being swollen, puffed up or overfilled. It is with this definition that we see, when it comes to people, the one thing that can bloat or puff up is the flesh. Therefore, it must be kept in check daily, or we may suffer the consequences.

As defined by Wiktionary, Bluto is a proper noun meaning "a man who is large and muscular in top-heavy proportions, often combined with a comically brutish and aggressive personality." When originally drawn, Bluto was an exceptionally large, bearded man with a serious weight issue. His girth far exceeded the measure of his chest, giving him a very sloppy appearance.

One of the problems Popeye faced when engaging Bluto in warfare was Bluto's choice of weapons: sheer brute force and tricks. His attacks were both physical and mental, with a particular focus on the latter. If he could catch Popeye with his guard down long enough to distract him, he had a chance to go after Olive Oyl and defeat Popeye for good.

As I watched this storyline unfold, I asked the question we should all be asking: "Didn't Popeye see this coming?" Time and again, Bluto would use the same gimmick. He would change the approach occasionally, but the results were always the same. Just as Popeye repeatedly fell for Bluto's tricks, too often, the Church falls prey to the Enemy's schemes. Doesn't the Church see what the Enemy is doing?

If so, why does it keep falling for the same gimmick each time? When is something going to change?

Popeye often allowed himself to be duped into situations that forced him into confrontation with his enemy. Sadly, many believers allow themselves to be drawn into similar yet avoidable situations. The Enemy, Satan, uses the same tactics that Bluto used against Popeye. His plan of attack is broken down into three stages: intimidation, assault, and robbery.

Whenever Bluto attacked Popeye, he always began with intimidation. He would mess with Popeye's mind by announcing his plan of attack and then following through with his threats. He would then assault Popeye, beating him down. Once the beating was over, he would complete the humiliation with robbery. Bluto often did this under the guise of friendship or as someone familiar to Popeye.

The Enemy consistently does the same thing to the body of Christ. He boldly tells us what he's planning to do and gives us a warning without expecting us to stop him. Then, he follows up with a hostile attack designed to make us throw in the towel and run for cover. While we argue among ourselves and retreat, he tries to make us abort the blessings God has bestowed on us and hand them over to be stored in the Enemy's camp.

Be incredibly careful of people who are in your life only to set you up to be defeated by the Enemy. They may seem real at the beginning, but appearances can be deceiving. This was often the case in Popeye's adventures, where he would start out as friends with Bluto, only to be tricked or betrayed later. On the other hand, true friends are there to celebrate you even if it is not their season of blessing as well.

Let us dig deeper into the Enemy's plan of attack. One by one, we will expose the truth of these battle plans. Keep in mind that you are stronger than any demon. They must bow to the name of Jesus that dwells in you.

INTIMIDATION

Intimidation is based on an individual's perception of self. It is only effective if the person has a low self-image and a diminished view of their role in Christ. The word "intimidate" as defined in Merriam Webster dictionary is as follows: Intimidate means to frighten, compel, or deter someone, typically through threats or by creating fear to influence their actions. It involves making someone timid or causing them to lose confidence period

We'll start with the first definition: "to make timid and to fill with fear." The only way someone can be made timid or filled with fear is if there is a lack of confidence in their own identity.

Satan cannot truly make something from nothing. He can only distort the truth to make it appear to be something that it is not. He can only offer you more than he has the capacity to deliver.

Christians must understand who they are in Christ. If we are indeed the sons of God and have become joint heirs with Christ, then why do we not operate in that truth? I am my Father's son. I know what is available to me through my name. I take advantage of my access because of who my Father is. Every Christian can do the same, and more, through their relationship with our heavenly Father. Know who you are.

Walk into that revelation. It is impossible to lack courage if you walk in the strength of your identity in Christ daily.

Fear is defined as a basic, intent, and often adaptive emotion aroused by the detection of imminent, real, or imagined danger (Dictionary.com, n.d.).

For God has not given us a spirit of fear, but of power and of love and of a sound mind.

(2 Timothy 1:7 NKJV)

The other part of the definition of intimidation is to fill with fear. Fear is not from God. It is an emotion based on a faulty belief. A common acronym for fear is False Evidence Appearing Real. If this is true, the evidence that leads to fear has no credibility whatsoever. Timidity is a cowardly fear, not being able to face a problem, but instead running from it. This often results from a lack of maturity.

Bluto would often use these two methods of fear against Popeye, who, in many episodes, appears timid when pushed to the point of confrontation. His fear does not come across as a phobia, which is an irrational, persistent fear or dread. Either way, this reflects the current situation in the Church. The Enemy uses both forms of fear: timidity and phobia to render the body of Christ impotent to the needs of the world. Many in the body of Christ hold tight to these types of fear with a bulldog-like grip, only relenting under severe pressure or death.

As a believer, you must trust that the Word of God is absolute truth. If you do, then you should walk in the truth that fear is not from God. It is an inherited curse resulting from the events in the Garden of Eden. Even so, we have the right not to claim that inheritance.

Many say that the opposite of fear is faith. I am not one of those people. I believe that the opposite of faith is sight.

Now faith is the substance of things hoped for,

the evidence of things not seen.

(Hebrews 11:1 NKJV)

If faith is defined by the Bible as "the substance of things hoped for and the evidence of things not seen," then sight must be the opposite of faith by default. To operate in faith is to believe. To not believe is simply doubt at its root. Doubt adds more power to the punch than you may think. Doubt, simply put, means to be unsure. If you are unsure, you are likely double-minded. Being double-minded leaves you open to a certain measure of fear.

There is no fear in love; but perfect love casts out fear, because fear involves torment. But he who fears has not been made perfect in love. (1 John 4:18 NKJV)

Fear not, for I am with you; Be not dismayed, for I am your God. I will strengthen you, Yes, I will help you, I will uphold you with My righteous right hand. (Isaiah 41:10 NKJV)

The LORD is my light and my salvation; Whom shall I fear? The LORD is the strength of my life; Of whom shall I be afraid? (Psalm 27:1 NKJV)

Yea, though I walk through the valley of the shadow of death, I will fear no evil; For You are with me; Your rod and Your staff, they comfort me. (Psalm 23:4 NKJV)

There are several Scriptures in the Bible that speak against fear because it can weaken our faith and cause us to doubt. Remember, if you operate in doubt, you will operate in defeat. You cannot be uncertain about the God you serve and lack confidence in the sacrifice of Christ while calling yourself a born-again believer. What do you truly believe in?

Bluto represents what I think is perhaps the greatest enemy of the Church today: the flesh. Not the tangible skin that can be touched, but the carnal mindset that many believers walk in daily—carnal, satanic, worldly flesh.

First the flesh intimidates you and floods your mind with propaganda; then it advances to a physical assault. When you are convinced by the propaganda and the false image is believed, defeat is often already secured. If the flesh can make you doubt your identity, all it needs to do is carry out its plan of attack.

Many are held down by this stronghold: being unwilling or unable to believe who they were created to be. The flesh would have you believe that you are less than you are. A carnal mind would have you believe that God is not for you. However, there is certainly more to you than you can see or imagine, even in your wildest dreams.

How did Jesus accomplish the many acts recorded and unrecorded throughout His time on Earth? Simple! He knew who He was and why He came to Earth. He did not doubt it. He did not have to ponder it. There was no wondering. He knew what the Father said about Him, and He operated fully in that faith.

Bluto the Terrible does not just represent the flesh; he also represents a mindset, specifically, a carnal mindset.

There is that word again: carnal, pertaining to the appetites of the flesh, the body, or the sensual, worldly and temporal, not spiritual. Did you catch that? The greatest enemy we must contend with is a carnal mindset. In the cartoon, Bluto never showed real love toward anyone. His attacks were often to keep Popeye away from Olive Oyl. He only wanted her as a trophy; he had no true feelings for her at all.

Sinful nature is something we inherit as a result of sin in the Garden of Eden. Every one of us is born into sin. However, developing and walking in a carnal mindset is often a choice, and it must be addressed to obtain and operate in the kingdom of God. All sin falls into one of three categories: the lust of the eye, the lust of the flesh, and the pride of life. The concept of sin is so dangerous that Jesus did not entertain the idea. There is no way He could have performed any of His miracles while walking in the flesh.

Jesus was able to perform miracles because He did not allow Himself to walk in the flesh. How was this possible? He had a different thought process. The Bible says that Jesus was tempted like us but without sin. It is possible to be tempted by the Enemy and not sin. After all, temptation is simply the presentation of a thought.

Is there any encouragement from belonging to Christ? Any comfort from his love? Any fellowship together in the Spirit? Are your hearts tender and compassionate? Then make me truly happy by agreeing wholeheartedly with each other, loving one another, and working together with one mind and purpose. Don't be selfish; don't try to impress others. Be humble, thinking of others as better than yourselves. Don't look out only for your own interests, but take an interest in others, too. You must have the same attitude that Christ Jesus had. Though he was God, he did not think of equality with God as something to cling to. (Philippians 2:1-6 NLT)

The very thought life of Jesus made the difference in all that He did. He was able to multiply fish and bread, walk on water, turn water into wine, heal the sick, raise the dead, and perform many other miracles simply because He knew, in His own mind, who He was and what that identity allowed Him to do. Every time you see a miracle being performed by someone, it is not because that person performed it on their own, but rather because they believed in God to perform it through them.

How did we get to this point of talking about miracles in a chapter dealing with the flesh? Simple. Operating in the flesh is ultimately a matter of the operation of your mind. Your thoughts and imagination are the key to unlocking the door of victory. We have seen Philippians 2:5 also translated as "have the same mind of Christ." I believe this is key to Christ's accomplishments.

Casting down arguments and every high thing
that exalts itself against the knowledge of God,

bringing every thought into captivity to the obedience of Christ. (2 Corinthians 10:5 NKJV)

Here, the word casting comes from the Hebrew word *chalaq*, which means to separate or to divide, to take away a portion, to set apart. The Word of God tells us to separate ourselves from all things that exalt themselves against the knowledge of God. This is not referring to the knowledge that God possesses. No human can even flicker a flame to the knowledge of God. Rather, this speaks about your personal knowledge of God. You must bring every thought into captivity. Every thought that denies you access to the Word and love of God must be apprehended. Every thought that would have you believe anything contrary to the Word of God must be cast down.

God has given us five basic senses: touch, taste, sight, smell, and hearing. These five senses, which most of us use daily, are the very tools that Satan preys upon to entice us into sin. Remember, Satan will pervert what God has blessed and turn it against Him. Practicing anything sensual outside of God's boundaries will lead to sin in your body.

The flesh (carnal mind) is the enemy that must be dealt with. Carnality does not refer solely to sexual matters. The Church has journeyed into a realm lacking moral restraint, where we allow the pleasure of our senses to take precedence over pleasing God. We would rather be entertained by worldly things than soak in the presence of God.

Carnality leads to materialism and covetousness, which we often attempt to justify with God's promises. Carnality feeds the sinful desire of man. Eventually, this leads to deeper and darker waters, resulting in being overtaken in a current of sin and death.

The LORD knows the thoughts of man, that they are futile. (Psalm 94:11 NKJV)

You will keep him in perfect peace,
whose mind is stayed on You, because he
trusts in You. (Isaiah 26:3 NKJV)

I say then: Walk in the Spirit, and you shall not fulfill the lust of the flesh. For the flesh lusts against the Spirit, and the Spirit against the flesh; and these are contrary to one another, so that you do not do the things that you wish. But if you are led by the Spirit, you are not under the law. Now the works of the flesh are evident, which are: adultery, fornication, uncleanness, lewdness, idolatry, sorcery, hatred, contentions, jealousies, outbursts of wrath, selfish ambitions, dissensions, heresies, envy, murders, drunkenness, revelries, and the like; of which I tell you beforehand, just as I also told you in time past, that those who practice such things will not

inherit the kingdom of God.

(Galatians 5:16-21 NKJV)

The danger of Bluto (the flesh) is that he focuses on the passions and appetites of sinful nature and the natural senses, rather than on the purity and holiness of God. We desire to see things our way and to hear only that which pleases us. We only want to smell aromas that are pleasing to our nostrils, drawn from our own choices and victories rooted in sin, rather than the aroma of our surrendered flesh in the nostrils of God. We want to taste forbidden fruit that allows our giftings to be prostituted, rather than to taste and see that the Lord is good. With unclean hands, we want to touch the very things that God has opposed instead of touching the heart of God in pure worship.

Since the Garden of Eden, the flesh has been elevated in places of worship—places God never intended. Bluto must be slain and placed on the altar daily. The Word of God tells us not to walk in the flesh.

But the fruit of the Spirit is love, joy, peace, longsuffering, kindness, goodness, faithfulness, gentleness, self-control. Against such there is no law. And those who are Christ's have crucified the flesh with its passions and desires. If we live in the Spirit, let us also walk in the Spirit.

(Galatians 5:22-25 NKJV)

And do not be conformed to this world, but be transformed by the renewing of your mind, that you may prove what is that good and acceptable and perfect will of God.

(Romans 12:2 NKJV)

CHAPTER 4

BRUTUS

THE BIG GUY WHO HATES POPEYE

NOW THAT WE'VE DEALT with Bluto and the flesh, let us address his tag-team partner and brother-at-arms: Brutus. By now, I am sure you have caught the flow of this book and realize that Brutus also holds a position against Popeye. Keep in mind that these characters are symbolic in nature. Popeye represents the Church, and Bluto represents the flesh, leading us to our third character in this cartoon series: Brutus. Brutus represents the spirit of the "strongman," sent to keep us bound in positions of sin and defeat, and to assassinate the character of every believer.

The name Brutus is most recognized in connection with Julius Caesar. In that story, Brutus was a Roman statesman and one of Julius Caesar's assassins. Much like Brutus in that story, the Brutus of the Popeye storyline has the same areas applied to this book. Brutus is set up not just as an enemy of Popeye, but also as one who seeks to assassinate the Church, not necessarily in a literal physical sense, but through plots against the name of Christ and the character in which every believer walks.

Brutus' role works hand in hand with the previously mentioned Bluto whose job is to get you to think incorrectly and operate in a carnal mindset. Brutus' job is to keep you there by any means necessary, hence, the connection with the "Strongman." The name Brutus has its origin in the word "brute." We have used this term to describe someone who is bully-like but let us take a closer look at it.

According to Dictionary.com, the definitions of brute are as follows: 1. a non-human creature, beast. 2. a savage, insensitive or crude person. 3. the animal qualities, desires etc., of humankind.

According to 2 Peter 2:12 and Jude 10, a brute is someone with animal-like qualities as is consistent with the definition given above. Look.

> *But these, like natural brute beasts made to be caught and destroyed, speak evil of the things they do not understand, and will utterly perish in their own corruption.* (2 Peter 2:12 NKJV)

But these speak evil of whatever they do not know; and whatever they know naturally, like brute beasts, in these things they corrupt themselves. (Jude 10 NKJV)

A "brute person" in the New Testament is referred to as someone who acts like a wild creature and speaks of things that they do not understand. They openly speak of natural things, not spiritual things. In order to get a fully accurate view of this, we must also take a closer look at the term "brute" as used in Old Testament Scriptures. In the Old Testament, the lines of usage are parallel to those in the New Testament. However, the term "brutish" takes on a slightly different meaning as it is used in a different context. It is here that we find the term used to mean a "foolish person."

For he sees wise men die; Likewise the fool
and the senseless person perish,
And leave their wealth to others.
(Psalm 49:10 NKJV)

O LORD, how great are Your works! Your thoughts are very deep. A senseless man does not know, Nor does a fool understand this. (Psalm 92:5-6 NKJV)

For the shepherds have become dull-hearted, And have not sought the LORD; Therefore they shall not prosper, And all their flocks shall be scattered. (Jeremiah 10:21 NKJV)

It is not by coincidence that the definition, as given by the absolute Word of God and the standard dictionary, describes the function of Brutus. He is an unwise, animal-like person who does not believe in the power of Popeye (the Church). Even though he knows that Popeye can overtake him, he is not discouraged by this knowledge. He revels in the fact that he can bully Popeye while believing that it will eventually lead to Popeye being bound in positions of impotence. It is here that the difference is made, as Popeye's response is not usually consistent with his confession. Brutus knows that he can manipulate our hero into a different position given the right stimuli and environment.

Why is the Church allowing itself to be manipulated out of its kingdom position by an enemy who is ultimately defeated? Yes, Christ has defeated Satan and every demonic imp that would dare to raise its head, but how many true believers walk in the liberty in which Christ has made us free to walk? Are you there yet? We must acknowledge the position of Brutus as the strong man. We are not talking about the guy at the fair wearing the leopard-print unitard with the curly mustache. Not at all. We are talking about the demonic spirit that is sent to try to keep you entangled in all your history. This position is so linked to the supernatural that even *Webster's Dictionary* defines the strong man with an unfavorable likeness:

1. Strong man: one who leads or controls by force of will and character or by military strength.

2. Statesman: a person engaged in fixing the policies and conducting the affairs of a government, especially one wise and skilled in such matters.

Here is where we recognize the "statesman" role of the strong man. He is designed to keep you in bondage to your past so that you cannot freely operate in the Spirit of God. It is in the role of a statesman that this spirit actively conducts the affairs of Satan's rule, working to keep believers from freely walking into their destiny. Yes, I know the Scripture says that where the Spirit of the Lord is, there is liberty. However, when someone is bound, there is no freedom to operate in any capacity, much less in the Spirit of the Lord.

Think about it: if your hands are bound and your feet are tied behind your back while you lie on your back, you are stuck in that position until someone sets you free. If the Enemy can keep you bound, you will never be able to move beyond that position and into your destiny.

So He called them to Himself and said to them in parables: "How can Satan cast out Satan? If a kingdom is divided against itself, that kingdom cannot stand. And if a house is divided against itself, that house cannot stand. And if Satan has risen up against himself, and is divided, he cannot stand, but has an end. No one can enter a strong man's house and plunder his goods, unless he first binds the strong man. And then he will plunder his house. (Mark 3:23-27 NKJV)

Here, Jesus acknowledged the Enemy as a strong man. But He also pointed to Himself as the "stronger man," being able to bind the "strong man." Now, just because Brutus was able to attack Popeye and bind him does not mean that the end was near for our beloved sailor. There is always a way out in Christ. God will provide a way out of the situation. However, in the meantime, while we are playing the games He never intended us to play the Devil sends demons to destroy our names and hinder the power of God's restorative love in our lives.

Brutus tried to assassinate Popeye's character and integrity—his honor and resolve. He constantly set trap after trap in Popeye's path, trying to bind him. He knew that if Popeye could avoid the traps and pitfalls, he would eventually become a true force to be reckoned with. Likewise, the spirit of Brutus puts obstacles in our path to make us fall, hoping that if we are reminded of past defeats and failures, we will never look beyond them and walk into our destiny.

Your past is the only leverage the strong man spirit has. He simply reminds you of a time when you did not walk in the love of God or in the power, He gave you to take dominion in the earth. Remember, the strong man is not a nice guy, and he does not play by the rules. Your bondage is his goal. However, he can quickly become a defeated foe. Every trap that Brutus set had the intention of either delay or death for Popeye. But regardless of the trap, Popeye somehow managed to grasp another chance at victory before it was all said and done.

Notice that the definition of "strong man" indicates that this spirit controls by force of will or character. Would you agree that, in this context, it is being said that this spirit controls either by the force of his will (the desire of Satan) over yours or by exaggerating his character over yours? The will of the strong man spirit is to see you bound and gagged, presented as unimportant to those around you, lacking in self-confidence, commonplace in appearance and function, irrelevant at best, and seemingly unable to operate in authority and power.

As I mentioned earlier, Brutus' job is twofold. He is not just a statesman; he is also an assassin—an agent of death. He is a murderer for hire whose purpose is to eliminate whoever is marked for death. His job is to murder by sudden or secret attack of the marked target.

You are marked for death. The Enemy is out to steal, kill, and destroy everything that has been marked by the blood of Jesus. That includes both you and me. He will stop short of nothing to accomplish this task. Brutus' job is to "still" you, to make you be still and unmovable.

How did Popeye overcome the schemes of the enemy? Ultimately, he had to be delivered from his flesh and from the hand of the enemy. He had to be set free from all bondage that was holding him back. Only when Popeye was free from bondage was he truly able to operate in the freedom of the spirit of liberty. Similarly, it is only when you, as a believer, are free from whatever trap the Enemy has set in your life that you are able to operate unrestrained in the fullness of the Godhead.

NOTES

CHAPTER 5

OLIVE OYL

SHE LOOKS GREAT for someone who has been around since 1919. That's right; Olive Oyl first came on the scene in 1919 as part of the Thimble Theatre comic strip. She appeared a full 10 years before Popeye did in 1929. Olive Oyl started out as a shy dancer and was engaged to Harold Hamgravy, who happened to have a passion for other women. This did not bode well for their relationship. Though she is most widely recognized as Popeye's gal, she and Popeye did not get off to the best of starts. They fought for weeks until they realized they had feelings for each other.

Though known as Popeye's love interest, Olive Oyl also plays the role of the damsel in distress. Her humdrum and plain outer appearance make her and Popeye seem like an odd couple. Her features only serve to further dwarf our hero sailor. Olive Oyl often gains the attention of many of Popeye's enemies, but her eyes are set on him as her first choice. What is it that this tall, slender, plain, and seemingly frail woman wants with Popeye? Even more important, what does he want with her? What is taking him so long to pursue her beyond this on-again, off-again courtship?

Olive Oyl is Popeye's intended and almost certain damsel in distress. But we cannot be fooled by what appears on the outside. There is much more to our dear Olive Oyl than meets the eye. Remembering the symbolism of the characters and their roles within our walk as Christians as it relates to this book, Olive Oyl embodies a threefold meaning that the Church must make a sound decision about. First and most obvious, Olive Oyl represents the anointing of God. Secondly, as thin as she is, she also represents the "fatness" of God. Thirdly, she represents the lost portion of the Church.

I knew immediately, in the early stages of this book, that Olive Oyl would have something to do with the anointing. Her name makes that clear. I was, however, totally unaware, and blown away, by her character representing the "fatness" of God. Before I get ahead of myself, let's deal with her gifts in due order. We must first deal with the anointing, and then we will transition into the fatness. Are you ready? Let's go.

The anointing! What is it? Where does it come from? Why do we need it? These three questions can be answered with one swift definition: The anointing is the burden removing and yoke removing power of God. It is what empowers people to function supernaturally. It enables you to do supernatural things. Verb (Anoint): to smear all over, rub into, pour all over (Wiktionary.com).

I would gander that most charismatics have a general understanding of “the anointing,” but how much do we really know about the “oil” and its role in the process? In the times of the Old Testament, there were many different oils in use for various reasons.

The oil used for anointing purposes was primarily made from olive oil, which was produced from olives, as the name implies. The processing of olive oil was not from pounding or crushing the olive, but rather from pressing. It was here that the olives were slowly pressed, resulting in the production of oil extracted from the fruit. The pressed olive oil would then be given to the hands of the perfumer, who would add spices to the olive fruit’s oil.

Now, pay close attention. Did you hear that? Though often mistaken for a vegetable, the olive is indeed a fruit. Think about the process of becoming fruitful, being chosen and then pressed to produce more than just the fruit itself. Sometimes, we get caught up in simply becoming fruitful. However, an entire dimension of productivity is waiting beyond fruitfulness.

There are three more words that we must define before going further. Please pay attention to these definitions as provided in the *Webster's New Dictionary of the English Language:*

1. Consecrate: to induct into an office with religious rite; to make or declare sacred; to devote solemnly to a religious or divine purpose.
2. Sacred: set apart for the service or worship of a deity; devoted exclusively to one service or use; worthy of veneration or reverence.
3. Service: the action of helping or doing work for someone.

The oil used for anointing is not plain or ordinary oil. It has been extracted from only mature olives. After harvesting, the olives are turned over for pressing or crushing to extract the absolute best of the oil within the fruit. Remember, the oil is given to the perfumer, who adds a mixture of spices to create the "perfect blend."

I find it interesting that in the Popeye storyline, Olive Oyl is often found in jeopardy, which causes Popeye to go into hero mode to rescue her. Together, Popeye and Olive Oyl can accomplish much more than either could on their own.

Popeye is drawn to Olive Oyl regardless of what may be at stake. She has an undying affection for our hero and is willing to overlook his obvious "shortcomings" because she still desires to be with him.

Much like our story, the anointing of God desires the Church to embrace it with no regard to the situation or circumstances of the present time. God is love, and as a result, He has made available to us, the body of Christ, a power to bring the realities of heaven into the earth realm. We must remember that the anointing is available to every believer, no matter how long you have been a Christian.

Though she may appear weak and powerless, Olive Oyl is strong enough to endure every obstacle without fail. She can overcome rejection, resistance, and being pushed away, only to be desired in the end. Olive can call upon Popeye with the confidence that he is on the way. He is equipped to deal with whatever enemy stands in the way. Remember, she can endure. She calls on Popeye, spurring him into action so that he can transform into who he is supposed to be. What is the anointing of God calling you to do? What are you being encouraged to become?

Christians are more than people who believe in God. They are those who have accepted Jesus Christ as Lord. They are ambassadors of Christ to the nations. Therefore, you are God's representative on the earth. As an ambassador, you have the backing of the country you represent—the backing of the One who sent you. The Word of God is our written executive order, and the anointing is our power of representation and authority in this earth. We must take hold of it and embrace the power available to us.

In Popeye's adventure, part of the problem is that he does not seem to embrace Olive Oyl until someone or something else seeks her affection. Likewise, many Christians do not pay attention to their God-given power on the earth until it is in jeopardy of being taken away or lost to another seeker of its presence. Don't get me wrong; many people know about the anointing, but they only seem to want to operate in it in the wrong type of environment.

Olive Oyl's intent was never to take anything away from Popeye. She only wanted to take what he had and multiply it. That is what the fatness of God is: increase. Fatness. She is the best, which means she exceeds all others. She is the rich portion, meaning she is abundant, containing much sweetness, richness, and depth. The best of the best. She is the lion's portion.

God wants the absolute best for you. He has chosen to provide that through His Son and His anointing. As a joint heir with Christ, you have definitive entitlements and benefits. However, it is your responsibility to come before God and discover what those benefits are.

The story of the prodigal son comes to mind. Do you remember how one son demanded his inheritance and squandered it living wildly? Afterwards, he found himself a broken and empty man, willing to return to his father as a servant. We've heard this story many times. Why did the father kill the fatted calf upon his son's return?

The emphasis should not be on the son and his return from defeat, but rather on the father. Yes, the father. The father recognized that his rebellious son had returned. The son repented before his father, turning away from all he had done. He desired to return to the life he had in his father's house. It was the father's responsibility to restore his son.

Definition of Restore (Merriam-Webster Dictionary)

1. To give back: return
2. To put back into use or service
3. To put or bring back into a former or original state
4. To put again in possession of something

Yes, it was the father's job to restore the son. What better way to do this and remind him of his value than to kill the best that he had? Like the Prodigal Son, we have all fallen away from God at some point in our lives. However, it is when we return to Him that He recognizes us and our repentance. Consequently, He replenishes us with the best He has to offer. Though the other son in the story deemed his brother unworthy of the best, the father did. Many of us do not think that we are worth the best, but we are because God has always given His best. He gave us Jesus.

Chapter 6

J. Wellington Wimpy

IN EXPERIENCING POPEYE in one way or another, I am sure everyone is familiar with one of the main characters: the one and only J. Wellington Wimpy. For the sake of familiarity, we will simply refer to him as Wimpy. There are no bones about it—they are buddies. Wimpy is seen throughout the series interacting with others on several different levels. The bottom line is that he is considered Popeye's friend.

Though Wimpy and Popeye are friends, it is a friendship of an unhealthy nature. As most people have learned in life, relationships like this will eventually take a toll on you. It is here that we begin our study of Popeye's friend and one of the biggest challenges facing the Church. Wimpy is a clear representation of slothfulness and gluttony.

Wimpy, like so many in the Church, is a well-educated man—so well-educated, in fact, that when the storyline first introduced him, he was considered "too" intelligent for the character's role as a professor. Essentially, he was given the responsibility of having no real job. He was cast more as a leech than anything else.

Wimpy's knowledge alone makes him capable of doing whatever he wants in life. He is not unlearned at all. So, you may ask, what is wrong with that? Here is the problem. We have learned so much about God, Jesus, and the Devil. We have learned the many names of God and how to use them. He is Jehovah-Jireh, my Provider; Jehovah-Shalom, God is my Peace. We have learned how to do church. We have learned the proper church lingo: "God is good all the time, and all the time God is good." We have been taught how to name it and claim it, blab it and grab it. We have learned how to be good church folk.

We have learned the history of the Church and our denominations. We have learned what matters and what does not. We've also learned the whimsical things of God. We have had great Bible teachers. We've purchased countless books, tapes, CDs, and still have VHS tapes hanging around. We have learned how to win souls for the kingdom, how to witness to others and the nations. We have even figured out how to fry the perfect chicken and fish to raise the money needed.

Most of us have "church sense." We have the ability to learn and understand church matters. And that is okay. But the question is: what are we doing with all of this knowledge? Where are we supposed to use all this great information we have learned over the years? Oh, I know—let us put it into practice in the church—the one place God really does not need our help. He has that covered with well-equipped shepherds called pastors. God never intended for the great resources He has provided for the world to remain behind the walls of the church.

Don't get me wrong; I am not saying go out and do whatever you want without accountability. No, not at all. What I am asking is: how much more do you need?

Wimpy's knowledge is enough for any business or trade. If he applied it, he could provide for himself as well as others. Instead, he has become a professional moocher, a leech, a con artist at best.

I give great credit to the many pastors teaching and equipping the body of Christ with the tools necessary for kingdom success. However, there are those who feed on the

Word of God and the blessings of others, never attempting to come into their own. I have been to churches throughout this country and around the world while in the military, and I have seen all kinds of things. The Church must deal with many people who have developed a parasitic anointing, spiritual leeches who feed off the anointing in other people's lives. They have no true desire to walk in or possess their own.

Why does Wimpy bargain with people when he has enough capacity to provide for his own needs? He is notorious for saying, "I'll gladly pay you on Tuesday for a hamburger today." I can understand someone needing help when they have just started out on this walk. I even understand generational curses that may be affecting you. I respect that; I have been there myself. But how long can you afford to remain a babe in Christ when there is a natural progression to walk as a Christian? What happens if Tuesday never comes?

Like newborn babies, you must crave pure spiritual milk so that you will grow into a full experience of salvation. Cry out for this nourishment. (1 Peter 2:2 NLT)

Here, we are given clear instructions that the milk is for a growing process. Once you have matured, you must eat the meat of the Word.

You have been believers so long now that you ought to be teaching others. Instead, you need someone to teach you again the basic things about God's word. You are like babies who need milk and cannot eat solid food. For someone who lives on milk is still an infant and doesn't know how to do what is right. Solid food is for those who are mature, who through training have the skill to recognize the difference between right and wrong. (Hebrews 5:12-14 NLT)

Wimpy is intelligent beyond comparison, but he is also lazy and gluttonous—a heart attack waiting to happen. A glutton is someone who eats in excess. Simple enough, right?

His girth symbolizes this nature but understand that one does not have to physically resemble Wimpy to be gluttonous. Keep in mind, he is symbolic. There are plenty of gluttonous people who look like Olive Oyl. Their high metabolism allows them to consume large amounts of food without gaining a pound. The same can be said about the Church, eating from table after table after table, consuming volumes of the Word, and never putting it to use.

I am not targeting anyone who is physically overweight or struggles with weight. I am targeting the spiritually morbidly obese. We are always "eating" the Word of God. As I said earlier in this chapter, we are constantly learning some new revelation or dimension of God. We eat, eat, eat, and eat! We belch and come back for more. We become so full on the Word of God that we lack the ability to exercise the very Word we have been chewing on. It is here that we become guilty of gluttony with the Word of God. Every Sunday service and midweek service is an opportunity to eat, but what do we do in return? Do we sit on it, waiting for it to manifest magically?

How can we continuously consume the Word and never become what we profess to believe?

We eat so much Word that we have 24-hour-a-day streaming buffets at our disposal. We have a smorgasbord of teachers and preachers from around the world. There is absolutely nothing wrong with having access to the Word of God. His Word shaped and formed the world in which we live. Personally, I enjoy being able to tune in anytime, anywhere, and receive what I need. My concern is that after consuming so much Word in so many flavors, what difference are we making in our communities, cities, states, and country? Why are we building so many prisons in this great Christian nation? Why are there so many abortions and divorces across this nation? Why is there so much wrong in a land where the overwhelming majority claim to know a God who is so right?

Are you ready for the answer? Are you sure? Okay, here it is: we have officially fulfilled the characteristics of J. Wellington Wimpy. We have become extremely lazy! There, I said it. We, the Church, overall, have become lazy in our walk with Christ. Some of us do not even walk with Christ anymore.

We ride behind Him on motorized ambition. Yes, I know there are those of you who have given tirelessly to the cause of spreading the hope of the gospel of Jesus Christ. But let us face facts: we have not pursued the lost at any cost.

Is this the Church Christ will return for? We, the Church, have reached a point where we must mature. How can we win people to a risen Savior if we do not do all that He requires of us? Yes, we enjoy the fun activities in church, but what about the work that must extend beyond the four walls—the activities that would draw the lost to call Christ Lord? We often encourage people to get involved in our programs, but to what extent are we willing to go to help them understand their true identity in Christ? What are we willing to do to help them fulfill their purpose in life? Why are our young people more interested in scripted reality than the Scripture of our reality?

Are we showing them the reality of living victoriously in Christ, or are they watching their parents go to church week after week while living a defeated life? Here is a radical statement: you cannot live a defeated life if you are truly living victoriously in Jesus. Wimpy is many things as a friend to Popeye, but he is even more of an enemy to the purpose of Popeye's life. It is the nature of Wimpy's presence that endangers the Church. When we operate in this spirit of laziness, we lose the attributes of Jesus, the Good Physician, and take on the persona of a modern-day Dr. Jekyll and Mr. Hyde. We are phenomenal on Sunday, living up to the expectations of those watching in the mirror. But when the lights are off and the doors are closed, we become Mr. Hyde, wreaking havoc in the lives of those we make our victims.

We have all had people in our lives like Wimpy—our friends, our families. However, we must keep these types of people at a distance. We must not allow spiritual parasites to feed off the anointing in our lives.

Chapter 7

The Sea Hag

THE SEA HAG is the most underrated enemy of Popeye. Though she was originally introduced as an enemy of Poopdeck Pappy, Popeye's father, she eventually became an enemy of our main character. Just as in our Christian walk, an enemy of our Father is indeed our enemy. The Sea Hag is exactly what her name implies. She is a witch! She is believed to possess charms or spells and have supernatural powers over natural forces. There is no doubt about her nature.

Although her contention began with Popeye's father, she became attracted to his son. In her attempt to draw Popeye out with spells, she was determined that if she could not have him to herself, then no one would. Yes, she knew about Olive Oyl, but she was no more concerned with her than with anyone or anything else. The key point here is that, regardless of the many disguises she assumes, she remains a witch with the same agenda and devices.

Keeping with the theme of this book, you have probably figured out by now that in this chapter, we will confront the fruit of Satan's sin in heaven. It was through his sin that we were introduced to rebellion. It is this satanic spirit that must be dealt with and destroyed in the Church today. Let us look at some definitions, from the Oxford Languages, Google Dictionary, that may give us a better understanding of these words:

Definition of Rebellion

1. An act of violent or open resistance to an established government or ruler
2. The action or process of resisting authority, control, or convention.

Definition of Stubborn

1. Having or showing dogged (tenacious or grim) determination not to change one's attitude or position on something, especially in spite of good arguments or reasons to do so.

Evil people are eager for rebellion, but they will be severely punished. (Proverbs 17:11 NLT)

The Church must crush the rebellion of the Enemy. Most rebellions are heard of in situations when there is an unjust ruler. The Church is not a democracy, nor is it a bureaucracy. It is a theocracy—a system of the kingdom of God set up on the earth by God Himself. Therefore, it is perfect in design. If there is an ungodly head of a church, that person should be replaced according to the Word of God, and healing should follow for the body. As for rebellion among the saints, there should be no question: God rules over this world.

With that being said, we must take a closer look at the short-lived reign of King Saul. Saul was Israel's first king. We will see the connection between rebellion and the Sea Hag by examining Saul's life. Take a moment to read 1 Samuel 15 in its entirety. Saul's rebellion began to surface prior to this point. It is here that we begin to see a blatant disregard for God and His sovereignty.

In 1 Samuel, you will read of the growth of the seer Samuel from youth to adulthood. Samuel ministered to God and eventually became a mature prophet unto Israel. This maturity led him into the presence of God when the people of

Israel demanded a king to rule over them. Though they already had a King in God, they insisted on a man to be king. Although Samuel was a proven and trusted prophet of God, the people insisted on a human king. Why do we insist on the same thing when it comes to our dreams, visions, and the operation of God in our lives?

After much prayer, Samuel anointed Saul the King of Israel as God had instructed. At first, Saul was very humble before God and ruled in accordance with His law. But in his second year as king, he began making decisions without seeking God's sovereign leadership.

Like Saul, many of us start our walk seeking God's active leadership, but at some point, we feel that we have become independent from Him while still being in Him. Saul made decisions and performed acts that elevated him above God's intention. The problem is that, as King of Israel, his primary responsibility was to please God and lead Israel to its destiny. Instead, he began promoting himself through acts of disobedience.

In 1 Samuel 13, Saul was instructed by Samuel to wait for him before going into battle. Under pressure, Saul realized that the men of Israel were fearful. They had completely lost heart when they saw the large number of enemy troops and began to run and hide. They hid in caves, holes, rocks, tombs, and cisterns. Some even left the battlefield completely. While this fear ran rampant in the army, Saul decided to step into a role he had not been ordained for, nor was he qualified to perform. He was king, but he assumed the role of priest by offering the burnt offering and peace offering himself.

It is striking that in the Church, there are many people who are anointed for one position but choose to force operations in other positions for personal gain. Saul should have waited on God and Samuel as instructed. Let us examine the result of his rebellion and the consequences of his disobedience. Just as Saul was concluding the burnt offering, Samuel arrived. The Bible does not say what caused Samuel's delay, and that is not the focus. What would have happened if Samuel had been a day later? No one knows, but Saul would have been better off waiting on God. Saul went to meet Samuel, who was upset because of what had been done. Upon inquiring, Saul's response was like that of many Christians:

> *But Samuel said, 'What is this you have done?' Saul replied, 'I saw my men scattering from me, and you didn't arrive when you said you would, and the Philistines are at Michmash ready for battle. So I said, "The Philistines are ready to march against us at Gilgal, and I haven't even asked for the LORD's help!" So I felt compelled to offer the burnt offering myself before you came.* (1 Samuel 13:11-12 NLT)

Wow, that is a lot to take into consideration. Like Saul, we are given simple instructions from God, yet we often act according to our own reasoning. How many times did Saul refer to doing something he wanted to do? He referred to his own wants and possessions seven times.

What makes this even more striking is that Saul never asked God for help until after the damage was done. Is this you? Do you make decisions that affect others without first consulting God? Here, the King of Israel was ready to lead his men into a war they were unprepared for, putting lives on the line without asking for God's help. Does this sound familiar? How many times have we made life-altering decisions without consulting God?

'How foolish!' Samuel exclaimed. "You have not kept the command the LORD your God gave you. Had you kept it, the LORD would have established your kingdom over Israel forever. But now your kingdom must end, for the LORD has sought out a man after his own heart. The LORD has already appointed him to be the leader of his people, because you have not kept the LORD's command.

(1 Samuel 13:13-14 NLT)

As a result of King Saul's disobedience, Samuel responded in an unpleasant way. Saul made the decision to move based on how he felt. He missed the mark. The start down a long, slippery slope was, no doubt, underway, with no intent on applying the brakes.

Though God used Saul's son Jonathan to lead Israel out of the situation with the Philistine army, Saul continued to make major decisions that would eventually lead to his downfall. He secured his position as king over Israel and continued to fight and make war constantly with the Philistines. It had come to the point that Samuel told Saul to go and destroy Amalek because of how they had come against Israel when they came up from Egypt.

The command was to destroy the entire nation of the Amalekites—every man, woman, and child. All cattle, sheep, camels, and donkeys were to be completely destroyed. This was the mission of Saul, King of Israel. He set out to accomplish it, mobilizing 200,000-foot soldiers and 10,000 men from Judah. However, somewhere between the time they left for the attack and the time Saul arrived at the battlefield, something in him changed. He warned the Kenites, who were living in the land of Amalek, to leave because they had been kind to Israel during their journey. 210,000 men had been sent to do battle, to perform the work of the Lord. They waited in a valley for the right moment, and when it came, they struck. But instead of completing the assignments given, Saul altered the Lord's command.

Then Saul slaughtered the Amalekites from Havilah all the way to Shur, east of Egypt. He captured Agag, the Amalekite king, but completely destroyed everyone else. Saul and his men spared Agag's life and kept the best of the sheep and goats, the cattle, the fat calves, and the lambs—everything, in fact, that appealed to them. They destroyed only what was worthless or of poor quality. (1 Samuel 15:7-9 NLT)

Here we go again! Saul was given a direct order from the man of God, and again, he decided to alter the plan. He was to destroy everything and everyone. He was not to keep anything. He had messed up so badly that God regretted making Saul king because of his disobedience and unfaithfulness. It grieved God that he had made Saul king.

Samuel the prophet cried out to the Lord all night. Early the next morning, he went looking for Saul and was told that he had gone to Mount Carmel to set up a monument to himself. When Samuel found Saul and inquired about the previous night's events, he could not believe what he was hearing. Saul felt as though he had done the right thing and had completely carried out the command of God. How can you be disobedient to the Word of God and try to offer as a sacrifice the very things He commanded you to destroy?

That is exactly what Saul did. King Agag and all those animals, as imperfect as they may have been, were never deemed good enough by God to be offered as a sacrifice. You cannot sacrifice to the Lord that which He has told you to destroy. There is no honor in such an offering. You have crossed into a curse instead of a blessing if this is the direction of your thinking. After all he had done, Saul still felt entitled to defend himself before the man of God. However, it was Samuel who told it plainly and clearly, as we should hear it today. This response was directed toward Saul's defense of his disobedience:

But Samuel replied, 'What is more pleasing to the LORD: your burnt offerings and sacrifices or your obedience to his voice? Listen! Obedience is better than sacrifice, and submission is better than the fat of rams. Rebellion is as sinful as witchcraft, and stubbornness as bad as worshiping idols. So because you have rejected the command of the LORD, he has rejected you as king.'

(1 Samuel 15:22-23 NLT)

Jesus is King of kings and Lord of lords. If He is King and Lord, we are also called to live as kings and leaders in His kingdom. We should never hear the call of God to take positions of rulership and then make Him sorrowful by our actions. Yes, Saul repented. However, even his repentance was consistent with his behavior and focused primarily on how he appeared before others rather than before God.

You have been called, and you are chosen. Why wait? Why be consumed with what others think when they have no authority over heaven or hell? There is absolutely no room for rebellion in the kingdom of God. Just as Popeye removes the threat of the Sea Hag, it is our responsibility to remove the threat of rebellion in the Church. Follow God's command to the letter, and you will not have to worry about offering what He has already rejected.

> *If someone claims, 'I know God,' but doesn't obey God's commandments, that person is a liar and is not living in the truth. But those who obey God's word truly show how completely they love him. That is how we know we are living in him.* (1 John 2:4-5 NLT)

NOTES

Chapter 8
Sweet
Pea

DO YOU REMEMBER that cute little baby who always garnered the attention of both Popeye and Olive Oyl? That baby was none other than Sweet Pea. His origin is somewhat mysterious as two different stories describe his beginnings. One suggests he came from a faraway land and was sent to be protected. Who really knows? His origins aren't important. What matters is that this adorable baby is symbolic of the youth of the Church.

Dealing with this chapter on Sweet Pea is of special significance to me. I have worked as a youth pastor throughout most of my Christian walk. I have faced many challenges and experienced great victories in seeing the true impact I have had on some of these lives. I realize that many within the Church have forgotten what it feels like to be young. Several of us have chosen to forget the challenges and perils of youth. Remember, you were not born an adult.

It is hard enough to be young today, but can you imagine how much more difficult it must be to grow up in a hostile environment? Can you imagine what it would be like to grow up constantly feeling judged by where you have been and what you have done? Can you picture being in an environment where what you are wearing is more important than the condition of your soul? Did you know that this type of environment is often found in the Church?

For many years as a youth pastor, I focused more on the rights and wrongs than on the condition of the hearts of our young people. Let me say without a doubt that I now realize this was wrong. I would often let my enthusiasm for God create a space in me that allowed me to be very stern, and oftentimes this came across harshly. So strong, in fact, that many young people were turned off and found it difficult to draw closer to the Lord. Not only were the youth turned off, but some parents as well. I would find myself frustrated and ask the million-dollar question: what did I do wrong?

I was a first-rate knucklehead! I was losing more young people than I was drawing to the kingdom, and I could not see where the problem was. Correction: I could see the problem and where it lay, but I was too comfortable with myself to make the change. However, as with most things in life, I had to check myself. I had to do so against a standard I expected these young people to meet, one that I often fell short of: God's standard. This is the sum of what I realized over the years.

We cannot blame our children for wanting to achieve more and go further than what they see in front of them. That is part of the natural progression of life from generation to generation, from glory to glory. As adults, we really cannot blame them for wanting fine jewelry, clothing, cars, and other material things. After all, we tell them that God wants the best for them, but if they only see worldly people living godly lifestyles and people of God who do not reflect the Word of God, who are they supposed to look to as an example? I know there are visible examples of godly blessings on earth, but are they so far removed from your children that they cannot relate to them?

We have set our children up for the Enemy to take them out! We tell them these great things, but we do not do enough to show them that the Word of God really works. When was the last time you were excited about the Word of God working in your life? Are you showing real joy and excitement about your relationship with the Father? I could ask questions until the cows come home, but the bottom line is this: we are setting the standard for the power of God in their lives.

I do not condone mischief, violence, or any of the bad things that people are into. I spent plenty of time doing all those crazy things as a youth. But are we really doing all we can as parents to raise our children in the way they should go? Is it easy? Of course not. However, we can make the experience much more pleasant if we do not compromise our own rules and identity in Christ. You will never see an example of God saying, "Do as I say and not as I do." Never! If God never did it, why do we think it is appropriate for us to do this to our children? We must change the way we present the gospel to young people. Today's youth are not blind. They are not living life according to a fairy tale. We must present the truth of God's Word in our lives first; then they will follow suit.

To every young person reading this book, I apologize on behalf of parents everywhere. Please forgive us! We have messed up. Please understand that somewhere, someone is acknowledging the gross misconduct of parents and adults everywhere. We have left you a mess that needs to be cleaned up.

In a world that desperately needs a true, living Savior, parents have been guilty of saying “Do as I say and not as I do,” not realizing that it is a standard of hypocrisy that we are setting. However, I do have good news. There is hope!

You see, in the storyline of Popeye, Sweet Pea appeared to be an infant child who was unable to really care for himself, and he barely had anything to say. He usually appeared incapable of walking and talking, but that was not the case. Like Sweet Pea, many of you have been treated like babies all your life, but there comes a time when you must grow up and fulfill your purpose on this planet. Maturity is a must—physically, mentally, and spiritually. God has given you gifts that are not for you but for the world.

Don’t let anyone think less of you because you are young. Be an example to all believers in what you say, in the way you live, in your love,

your faith, and your purity.

(1 Timothy 4:12 NLT)

This Scripture provides the basis for how young believers in Christ must operate if they are to change the culture and context of the Church and succeed in God. Let's break it down.

- **Do not let anyone despise your youth.**

  The word "let" simply means to give permission. Do not give the world permission to look down on you. In that, you must make sure you do not give them a reason to. As the saying goes, if it walks like a duck, quacks like a duck, and looks like a duck, chances are it is a duck. Walk upright before all men, and you will never have reason to walk in shame.

- **Be an example to other believers.**

  Though Paul was exhorting Timothy, a young man in

ministry, he referenced the believers in the Church. You have so much more to contend with today than when I was your age. There are believers in the Church and people outside the Church as well. You must contend with those who believe in you and share your dreams, as well as those who believe you are a waste of time and will end up going nowhere. Be an example. Be the model to be followed, not the model to be avoided.

How are you to be the example? In a time when it is so easy to go in the opposite direction of what is expected of you, you must be an example in word and in conduct. There are six points that must be understood and embraced to become who you are meant to be.

1. WORD – something that is said, especially a brief remark or special revelation from God.
   As a Christian, it is imperative that you keep your word and the Word of God. Your kept word will take you places that a broken word will only leave you

dreaming about. Keep your word. Never enter a contract you do not plan on keeping. Count the cost before you begin anything.

2. CONDUCT – management, direction; behavior.
   If you act like a clown, expect clown rewards. Do not expect anyone to take you seriously if you do not take yourself seriously. There is no honor among thieves, and a clown will always be laughed at. How you conduct yourself says a lot about who you are and the direction of your life. Who wants to follow someone who does not know where they are going?

3. LOVE – unselfish, benevolent love for others.
   John 3:16—you know it well. Even non-believers quote this Scripture as a reference for love. For God so LOVED the world that He gave… PERIOD. It is okay to love. I am not talking about sexual love, but I am talking about benevolence. You know, an act of

kindness, charity. It takes more energy not to walk in love than it does to freely walk in the love of God.

4. SPIRIT – essential or real meaning; intent.

   Always be pure in heart and intent. There is an old saying I remember from my early days as a Christian: "The road to hell is paved with good intentions." I cannot say that it is Scripture, but the Word of God discerns the thoughts and intents of the heart. Do not set out to do anything with evil motives. God is looking at your heart.

   "For the word of God is alive and powerful. It is sharper than the sharpest two-edged sword, cutting between soul and spirit, between joint and marrow. It exposes our innermost thoughts and desires" (Hebrews 4:12 NLT).

5. FAITH – allegiance to duty or a person; belief and trust in God.

Know who you serve and why. Be sure of why you serve and trust in God. Do not just know about Him; get to really know Him. Become intimate with God and desire to please Him in all that you do. There is a void in you that only the presence of God can fill. Unfortunately, we often try to give the adoration and love meant for God to a substitute that cannot compare. Remember, He is a jealous God.

6. PURITY – the quality or state of being pure.

   Purity is not just about sexual conduct. You must be free from anything that violates, weakens, or pollutes your mind or spirit. Stay clear of moral fault and decay. You cannot mix the world with God and expect to remain godly. You will drift to one or the other, not both. It is daunting to think people may pray for something and then use worldly concepts once God has blessed them.

Remember, you are the standard by which everything in your life will be measured. When God made you, He had the world in mind. You are the solution to someone's problem. Inside of you are gifts He has given for the world. Will you believe that you are special and the whole earth is awaiting your arrival? Will you begin your search for the truth of who you are in Him? His truth trumps your truth on any given day. Will you exceed the limitations others place on you? God created you to be great. Trust Him. He did not make a mistake. He is God!

Chapter 9

Spinach the Word

SPINACH

SPINACH

SPINACH

OKAY, WE HAVE COME THIS FAR and have yet to touch what is perhaps the most renowned connection to Popeye. No matter the episode, foe, or situation, this is one of the common denominators of every episode: the source of his super strength—SPINACH! But I must correct the common misbelief that Popeye's strength came from the spinach he ate. There are plenty of episodes that show him using great strength before consuming the great green veggie.

Popeye's strength is not completely based on his consumption of spinach. You may disagree and say, "Hey, I distinctly remember seeing Popeye eat spinach to get strong." You would be partially right. The increase in strength was not in the spinach alone; it was coupled with his recognition of the word "spinach."

Let us talk about this leafy green vegetable for a moment. Spinach is rich in vitamins A and C and various minerals such as iron and riboflavin, which is a B-complex vitamin. Vitamin A is required for especially good vision, while vitamin B and the B complex are essential for the normal function of certain enzymes and for growth. Vitamin C is needed by the body to prevent disease and build the immune system. Rounding out the benefits is riboflavin, a growth-promoting vitamin in the B family. Spinach also contains fiber, folic acid, and other nutrients that help fight colon and breast cancers, high blood pressure, and heart disease. We will return to the importance of these benefits in just a short time.

During the research for this book, I watched almost every episode of Popeye available—early cartoons, later versions, and everything in-between. All pointed to spinach, or rather, the word "spinach." Whenever Popeye was in a bind, he would either produce, out of thin air, a can labeled "spinach," or he would find some fresh spinach nearby. Even in his search for spinach, whether canned or fresh, he always recognized that the strength to overcome his issue was within the word "spinach." It empowered him to break the bonds of his oppressors and walk into victory.

In one episode, there were several canned goods around, and Popeye would only gain strength when he partook of the one with the word spinach written on it. Though the original concept was to promote the consumption of spinach by children, God knew that when Popeye was created, one day many years later, you would be reading this book.

Just like Popeye, as Christians, we must first recognize that the Word of God is the highest authority in the land. It is the Word of God that the foundation of creation rests upon. All that ever was, is, or ever will be is based upon the Word of God. Everything that exists is established upon God's Word.

In the beginning was the Word, and the Word was with God, and the Word was God. He was in the beginning with God. All things were made through Him, and without Him nothing was made that was made. (John 1:1-3 NKJV)

Popeye recognized that within himself he did not have enough power to overcome his enemy. He realized that he was in a position that required more power than he could muster and more skill than he possessed. In this, he understood that the word contained the power and authority that he needed in order to be victorious in his current situation. We, too, must recognize that the Word of God contains enough power to establish and maintain an entire universe without our assistance.

Life as it was in the beginning, as it is now, and whatever may be in the future is all held together by the Word of God. The Word is synonymous with the person of Jesus. Before He was called Jesus on the earth, He was the Word in heaven.

Popeye is seen buying spinach, napping by fields of spinach, and even planting gardens of spinach throughout the cartoon. We have seen him strongly encourage his nephews to partake of spinach as well. However, one of the challenges I have observed is that he never partakes of the green power food until something drastic happens. We do not see him eating it consistently unless there is trouble in the camp.

Many Christians maintain this same mentality as Popeye. We know that there is power and deliverance in the Word of God, but we do not search the Scriptures until there is a dire need for God's help. Perhaps the problem is that the average believer does not know the power of God on a personal level.

As I already mentioned, the first step to accessing God's strength is to recognize His Word for what it is: POWER! Sheer, unadulterated power. The second step is to consume, or eat, the Word of God for benefit. You must try it for yourself to understand exactly what is available to you.

Oh, taste and see that the LORD is good.

Blessed is the man who trusts in Him!

(Psalm 34:8 NKJV)

After you have eaten of the Word as Popeye does, you must then receive the benefits of what you have consumed and all its power. It would do you no good to work all week, receive your paycheck, and never deposit it so you can use the money for what you need.

And the Word became flesh and dwelt among us, and we beheld His glory, as of the only begotten of the Father, full of grace and truth. And of His fullness we have received, and grace for grace. (John 1:14, 16 NKJV)

Imagine starving yourself to the point of death. I mean really to the point of death. Then you eat just enough to survive, and once you have begun to recover, you start the process all over again. Starving yourself again. Imagine the injury that you would inflict upon yourself and the changes you would go through by not eating the proper food on a regular basis. Do you get the visual picture of going through that process? How much strength is in that?

Just as natural food has its benefits, there are benefits to eating the Word on a daily basis. The Word of God will give you direction and strength to endure. It will give you knowledge and understanding, wisdom in times of need, and peace in times of the storm. The Word of God gives you joy in times of sorrow and courage in times of fear. The Word of God cannot fail!

I mentioned in the beginning of the chapter that spinach is rich in vitamins A, C, and various minerals. It is especially high in iron and riboflavin. This green leafy vegetable is an excellent source of strength for Popeye. The Word of God is the only source of required nutrients to be a well-balanced believer. Just as vitamin A is required for good physical vision, the Word of God is necessary for good spiritual vision as well. Look at these Scriptures:

> *Your word is a lamp to guide my feet and a light for my path.* (Psalm 119:105 NLT)

> *At that very time, Jesus cured many people of their diseases, illnesses, and evil spirits, and he restored sight to many who were blind.* (Luke 7:21 NLT)

And Jesus said, "All right, receive your sight! Your faith has healed you." Instantly the man could see, and he followed Jesus, praising God. And all who saw it praised.

(Luke 18:42-43 NLT)

Jesus healed blind people on the way to Jericho and, when He was leaving, made sight a number one priority. The Word of God has enabled blind people to see, both naturally and spiritually, throughout the annals of time. Perhaps one of the issues facing the Church today is the belief that seeing is believing. When it comes to faith, not seeing strengthens it, allowing for the manifestation of God's power and provision.

Spinach is also rich in vitamin C, which is known to help build strong and healthy immune systems. The immune system protects the body from foreign substances, cells, and tissues by producing an immune response. It helps your body fight off infection and disease whenever needed.

The Word of God is an offensive and defensive weapon that is equally formidable. It will keep you from succumbing to spiritual attacks. Notice that I did not say it will keep you from being attacked. You will face trials and tribulations, but even in those trials, there is power in the Word of God to help you overcome any test. No test, no testimony.

For the word of God is alive and powerful. It is sharper than the sharpest two-edged sword, cutting between soul and spirit, between joint and marrow. It exposes our innermost thoughts and desires. (Hebrews 4:12 NLT)

Spinach is rich in riboflavin, a growth-promoting vitamin of the B Complex. The Word of God will cause growth in your life. It will become everything you need it to be to grow and mature in your spiritual walk. As a new believer, or a babe in Christ, you learn Scripture basics that will establish you in your walk with Christ. That is the milk that every new form of life must have. But when you have matured, you transfer from milk to meat. The meat of the Word of God is for mature

Christians to build strong and healthy spiritual immune systems.

Iron, a magnetic chemical element found in nature, is a main part of spinach. It is essential for the transport of oxygen in the blood and is part of some enzymes needed for the restoration of damaged cells. Whenever Popeye eats spinach, a chemical reaction takes place in his body, enabling extra oxygen to be delivered to the blood. It is the sudden and powerful restoration of these damaged cells that enables him to break free from what has kept him bound.

The Word of God, when eaten daily, will restore any damage in your life and will absolutely allow you to receive the power needed to break the bonds of any enemy. It is when Popeye recognizes the power of what is in the spinach he eats that he begins to comprehend the power of the recognized word. You must recognize the Word of God and the power that dwells within.

NOTES

Chapter 10
Profession

Profess is to openly declare, affirm, or claim something, often - though not always - and sincerely or falsely.

KEEPING IN STEP with our previous chapters, we have come to the conclusion of the matter. We began this book by talking about Popeye's physical appearance and then his confession. We have dealt with the issues of the flesh and spiritual strongholds in the chapters dealing with Bluto and Brutus. We went on to discuss the best that God has for you and its fatness in Olive Oyl. We preceded to deal with the issues of laziness through Wimpy and rebellion in the Sea Hag. Sweet Pea taught a valuable lesson for our youth and the power of the Word of God in that great leafy green vegetable spinach.

It has come down to this. The culmination of everything leads to Popeye's profession. Did you realize that there is a difference between a confession and a profession? Yes, there is a difference. Interestingly, many people think that they are one in the same. They are not. Let me remind you that a confession is, usually but not always, an acknowledgment of guilt. A profession, however, is an open declaration or vow of a belief or opinion. In short, a negative confession condemns you while a godly profession sets you up for promotion.

Once Popeye has partaken of the spinach and received the strength to break out of his chains, he can defeat his enemy. In doing so, He comes forth with two very strong professions of faith that, if you apply them to your life, will change the shape of your world. We will deal with these in reverse order.

After defeating his foe and saving Olive Oyl from certain doom, Popeye sings the words “I'm strong to the finish cause I eats me spinach. I’m Popeye the sailor man!” He has just defeated his foe, and he knows that he is indeed strong enough to make it to the finish line. The reason? He ate his spinach. Remember, he recognized the word “spinach” as his authority and strength. Here, we see Popeye and know that he is victorious and strong because of his spinach. As a believer, if you are ever going to defeat your enemy and walk in total victory, you must make the declaration that you believe the Word of God is true. We may never get to see Popeye eat spinach before trouble arrives, but I encourage you to eat God's Word daily.

God sent Jesus to be the perfect propitiation for sin. Yet, the world is still in need of a refreshing—the gift of God that He has placed within your life. I am not saying that you must become the next great TV evangelist or musician. You may not be called to that level, or to be an international businessman. I cannot tell you why you are here on this planet; only God knows that. But I can tell you this: you, yes, you, were bought with a price too high for you to never step into your purpose and fulfill your destiny on this earth.

Do not settle for mediocrity. Being okay is not okay. It is time to stand in front of God, walk forward in the promise, and deliver that baby that has been sitting in your spirit since before time began. Your destiny is calling, and someone, somewhere is waiting for you to bring forth the fruit God planted in you. The world needs you. It does not matter what anyone has said. God put something phenomenal inside you, and it is time for you to shine. Do not deprive the world of the opportunity to get to know God through you. The gift is not you but rather the gift of God in you.

If Popeye can finally recognize who he is and walk in his authority, surely you can do the same. You can become who you are really purposed to be. I know who I am and whose I am. I know why I am here for this day and time. I am walking in my purpose. You might ask the question that so many have asked in the past: who do you think you are? My answer is quite simple: "I y'amz what I am."

ACKNOWLEDGEMENTS

First and most importantly, I thank **GOD**! He gave me the idea for this book and continues to direct my life. If anyone receives anything from these pages, all glory belongs to Him.

I thank my wife, **Yoshica**. Without your encouragement and support, this book would still be on the back burner of life. Through every "gentle" nudge and every encouraging word, we have finally made it here.

To my daughters, **Shaundrieka** and **JeLia**, thank you for allowing the healing and growth that helped push this project forward.

To my **mother**, thank you for your many years of support, even when you didn't fully understand my vision.

To my **brother** and **sisters**, thank you for the push.

Bishop Richard Jennings, my brother and my friend—without you, sir, there wouldn't have been a trip to take or a place to receive the download. **Mother Alice Jennings**, that call pushed me through.

Thank you to **Mariesa Moore-Gentry** and **Your Best Dash® Publishing**. God chose you for such a time as this.

I would like to sincerely thank the pastoral leaders who have helped shape and strengthen my walk with Christ from 1994 to the present:

To **Bishop Steven L. Williams** and **Dr. Marlene Williams** of Lord of the Harvest Christian Fellowship Center (North Charleston, SC), thank you for allowing me the space to birth and develop the artistic gifts God placed within me. Your leadership provided room to grow and loving correction when it was needed.

To **Pastor Kenneth Gerald** of Oasis Church Charleston, thank you for cultivating an environment where I began to truly learn how to rest and recover in God. It was there that I came to understand what it means to genuinely "Love God and Love People."

To **Pastor Duaine Johnson** of Dominion LA, thank you for the many conversations, encouragement, and push to release what God placed within me and to "Be All That God Has Ordained." I believe Los Angeles will be greatly impacted through your ministry and leadership.

To **Apostle Ron Carpenter** and **Hope Carpenter** of Redemption Church, thank you for the tremendous Kingdom impact you have had on our lives. From my very first Redemption experience, I knew I had found my tribe. It is through your ministry that I have grown in my understanding of the Kingdom of God and been challenged to pursue the depths of God's desire and purpose for my life.

Thank you all for your prayers, leadership, wisdom, and obedience to God. Your influence has left an enduring mark on my spiritual journey.

Lastly, a very special thank you to a very **special group** of people. Without your prayers, your time, and your seeds of love, this book would still be a "maybe one day" project.

CONNECT WITH THE AUTHOR

Thank you for taking this journey with me. My prayer is that something in these pages helped you see yourself more clearly through God's eyes.

If this book spoke to you in any way, I would love to hear from you. Feel free to reach out, share your thoughts, or simply connect. Let's continue growing together.

Stay connected:

Email: SDRussellArt@Hotmail.com
Website: www.SDRussellArt.net
TikTok: SD Russell Art
Instagram: PerceptionsOf
Facebook: SD Russell Art

www.ingramcontent.com/pod-product-compliance
Lightning Source LLC
Chambersburg PA
CBHW060937050726
47592CB00003B/995